BEATRICE
LOSES HER DOLL

Written by Pam Halter
Illustrated by Kim Sponaugle

"If a man owns a hundred sheep,
and one of them wanders away,
will he not leave the ninety-nine on the hills
and go to look for the one that wandered off?"
Matthew 18:12

Beatrice looked under her bed.

She checked the closet.

She searched through the toy box.

DOLLY WAS NOWHERE TO BE FOUND!

Beatrice sat down on the floor. Where could she be?

Beatrice remembered learning about the lost sheep in Sunday school. Her teacher had told them that a shepherd looks and looks until he finds any sheep that is lost.

Beatrice thought, "It would be fun to dress up like a shepherd. Then I could look for Dolly until I find her!"

She went to the hall closet and pulled out a towel.

Taking the belt from Daddy's bathrobe,
Beatrice tied the towel on her head.

Beatrice went down the hall. She checked in the hamper.

She peeked into the bathroom.

Then she went downstairs and looked behind the TV ...

... and under the couch.

She dug through the kitchen trash can— just in case—but
DOLLY WASN'T ANYWHERE!

"I wonder if Dolly went outside," thought Beatrice. She looked out the window. "I'll check out there next."

Elliott popped his head up over the fence. "Whatcha doin',
Beatrice?" he asked.

"Looking for my lost sheep," stated Beatrice.

"You look funny," said Elliott. Beatrice tossed
her head. "Shepherds look EVERYWHERE for their lost
sheep, and I am looking EVERYWHERE
for Dolly," she said.

19

And with that, she stomped all the way back to the house!

As she opened the door, Beatrice wondered if she would
EVER see Dolly again!

Suddenly, she spotted a familiar blue dress in the laundry
basket. "DOLLY! I FOUND YOU!" she cried.

Beatrice hugged Dolly tightly.

Later, when she was having a tea party with Dolly, Beatrice thought about shepherds and "lost sheep."

"It must feel awful to be lost," she said. "And shepherds must get really tired sometimes."

Beatrice poured some tea into Dolly's cup. Then she remembered when her pastor had said, "Jesus is our Good Shepherd. He doesn't want anyone to be lost from Him."

"I sure am glad that Jesus found me!" she said. "He never gives up looking when one of His sheep is lost. He doesn't get tired either."

"He's the best Shepherd of all," she added.

Dolly silently agreed.

Hi kids!

Do you know that we are all Jesus' sheep? He is our Good Shepherd. He takes care of us and He never gets tired. Jesus loves each and every one of us. He died on the cross for all the bad things we do called sins. Everyone who believes that Jesus died and rose again will live with Him forever in heaven.

The lost sheep are the ones who don't know that Jesus loves them, or don't want to believe that He